Echoes of th

GREAT WESTERN

R. J. BLENKINSOP

© 1973 Oxford Publishing Co.

SBN 902888 32 3

Printed by B. H. Blackwell (Printing) Ltd
in the City of Oxford

Published by:
Oxford Publishing Co.
5 Lewis Close
Risinghurst
Oxford

Photo reproduction and offset plates
by Oxford Litho Plates Ltd.

PREFACE

The photographs in this book follow on in chronological order by date from my previous book 'Shadows of the Great Western' and cover the period October 1956 to May 1958. I tend to look at these years as the best for photography on the main lines, as many of the trains were clean and an intensive steam service was run, although the diesels were well on the horizon. The performance of the Great Western engines was at its best and it is sad that I could not have spent more time on what was a very absorbing hobby. Looking back I regret that my travels did not go into Wales more often and that my cover of the branch lines and freight trains was insufficient. This comes about as the challenge of photographing the fast moving trains was enormous and armed with the necessary permits I could visit the lineside when perhaps others could not.

When I first started railway photography I soon learned that the basic requirement was a fast shutter speed to stop all movement. After experimenting with a variety of Roll film cameras (6 x 9 cms) they all suffered from a variety of faults and it became obvious that, as I could not afford a professional plate camera, the only alternative was to make one. This may sound ambitious but I had recognised the few essentials i.e. large negative, good lens, focal plane shutter, necessity for the film to remain flat and in the same position for each picture, solid construction and open frame viewfinder.

I purchased an old Zeiss plate camera and built a plywood extension onto the focal plane shutter body, and fitted to the front panel a Ross Xpres lens in a focussing mount.

A wire frame viewfinder was constructed and a roll film holder taking 120 film was used instead of plates. The results you can see in this book but of course I have not included the failures of which there were many. My specification was met in all departments except the fourth which on reflection is a pretty important one and became so bothersome looking at negatives with some parts out of focus, that by 1960 I had gone over to 35mm for reliability and reduced cost, but that story is yet to come. I used exclusively Ilford film No. 120 H.P.3. and developed in

Promicrol to give extra film speed and detail in the shadows. It may be of interest to some readers that my printing technique for the Oxford Publishing Company method of printing has had to be completely changed to give the necessary liveliness in reproduction.

I have pointed out in this book many items of interest in the captions but one of the enjoyments for the reader is to find odds and ends which I have missed.

A number of you will have been on the special trains shown in this volume and it is my loss that I could not be with you, but in the final analysis I think I made the right choice. Many specials were run in this period and we should be grateful to British Rail for all the arrangements they made and history is now repeating itself with the second year of 'Return of Steam' just commencing at the time of writing.

In my first book a number of pictures were shown taken in Devon and I make no apology for more in this book as the most interesting engine work occurred over the Devon inclines and the country is so attractive.

I well remember on one occasion being unable to find a hotel for the night and having to sleep in the back of my Morris Minor with the back seat removed and feet sticking into the boot. Before going to sleep I opened the driver's window and locked the car from the outside and then replaced the keys in the ignition switch. After a rather uncomfortable night I woke early, and as I was off the main road, got out in my pyjamas to have a stretch. The door slammed shut and I was locked outside with the keys safely inside the car. I shall leave the reader to work a solution to this problem which was solved after an hour with judicious use of various pieces of wood.

On another occasion between Teignmouth and Newton Abbot I pulled into a lay-by and rushed down an embankment to catch the 'Cornish Riviera Express' and, on returning, did not notice there was a low metal seat just in front of the car. I started away and the edge of the seat went straight through the radiator with obvious consequences.

I hope you enjoy another fiesta of steam engines recalling the everyday scene of how we travelled in the days of steam.

1 This special train ran from Paddington to Stratford-upon-Avon, calling at Leamington for both engines to take on water. It was the first visit to the United Kingdom of the Russian Ballet dancers, starting a succession of cultural exchanges. No. 5060 **Earl of Berkeley** and No. 5065 **Newport Castle** are between Leamington and Warwick. Notice the two types of 'Castle' chimney, the older type having an extra three inches on the central parallel part of the casting.

21 October 1956

2   2-6-0 No. 6331 climbs slowly up the bank to Harbury with an up freight on a bright winter morning. I was standing on the buffer stop at the end of the down loop at Fosse Box as No. 6006 **King George I** swept by at over 80 m.p.h. with the 11.10 Paddington -Birkenhead express. This kind of situation so infrequently happens but calls for quick thinking and pressing the shutter release at the correct moment. Even with a shutter speed of 1/1000 second the tender is blurred.

29 December 1956

3   This picture was taken on a freezing winter morning with the sun almost head on. The 10.00 Birmingham-Paddington express approaches Leamington Spa G.W.R. shed and is about to pass over the Warwick and Napton Canal behind No. 5047 **Earl of Dartmouth**. Apart from the 'up main' which is off, the other two signals control entry into Leamington shed and carriage sidings. An illuminated speed restriction board gives warning of the speed allowed over the down fast and slow lines in Leamington Station.

2 March 1957

4

I always thought the 'Counties' were handsome looking engines particularly when viewed from the side. Having just passed Warwick Gas Works, and the fireman taking a rest, No. 1024 **County of Pembroke** attacks Hatton Bank with the Margate-Birkenhead 'through' train.

9 February 1957

5

Sunday engineering maintenance often produced interesting working. The morning Birmingham-Paddington train has just reversed over the down line at Fosse Box and starts away South to Banbury. No. 6001 **King Edward VII** is in charge and the driver has helped with a request smoke effect which hangs over 2-8-0 No. 3839 standing in the up loop, with a coal train. A 2-6-2T is in the down loop awaiting to go on to Leamington.

3 March 1957

6 Running into Paddington, a 'Brittania' Pacific No. 70026 **Polar Star** has completed its morning work with the 'Capitals United Express' from Cardiff. This was the engine involved in the derailment which occurred on 20 November 1955 at Milton near Didcot. One of the recommendations in the report was to improve the driver's visibility and this led to the removal of the handrails on the side of the smoke deflectors. One can clearly see the rectangular holes let into the smoke deflectors to provide access to the running plate so improving the driver's vision. Note the double-sided water column and shunter's cabin alas all now removed.

23 March 1957

7 For a short time the 'Cambrian Coast Express was worked by locomotives of the 'County' class and here No. 1017 **County of Hereford** leaves Paddington with the train in Great Western livery. It was also unusual for the headboard to be missing on this train.

23 March 1957

8 0-6-0 Pannier Tank No. 9400 brings empty stock into Paddington Station. The train comprises an N.E.R. luggage van and a rake of standard Great Western suburban coaches. This engine now sits peacefully in Swindon Museum for all to remember.

23 March 1957

9 Both engines shown here are of the 'Hall' class but No. 4993 **Dalton Hall** which leads is in black livery and the one behind in Great Western green. If any reader could help identify the second engine I should be most grateful. The arrival time was around 11.30
23 March 1957

10 This was always a difficult location to obtain a good photograph of the 'Cornish Riviera Limited' as the sun was non-existent behind the station buildings on the right. The train is shown leaving behind No. 6026 **King John**, at that time shedded at Plymouth Laira. The attraction of this photograph, is father showing son the marvels of steam and one wonders if he can remember it now he is grown up. Another 'King' moves empty stock in the background.

23 March 1957

11 A modified 'Hall' No. 7920 **Coney Hall** leaves Platform 1 with an express for Cheltenham. In front of the engine can be seen N.E.R. stock standing in the parcels bay.
23 March 1957

12 A dull wet day marred this picture of the first annual special train from Paddington to the Festiniog Railway Society Annual General Meeting at Portmadoc. However, No. 5040 **Stokesay Castle** was nicely turned out for this trip by the staff at Old Oak Common and a suitable headboard is attached to the smokebox. The location Hatton Bank.

30 March 1957

13 This is perhaps a rather orthodox picture of No. 6014 **King Henry VII** on the 09.00 Birmingham-Paddington, but I wished to include the splendid wooden home signal on the down line, outside the Harbury Cement Works.

6 April 1957

6 April 1957

14 Signals and trackwork abound in this photograph of No. 1022 **County of Northampton** passing through Warwick with the Ramsgate-Birkenhead train, which ran throughout the year. In Warwick Station can be seen the 2-6-2T banker which stands on call for any train requiring help up Hatton Bank. The up signals hang down in typical Great Western fashion; it must be more than 45 degrees!

6 April 1957

15 2-8-0 No. 2851 is fresh from an overhaul but appears to have been cleaned at Tyseley before the day's work. With the regulator just open, it is slowly approaching Leamington with a down freight. The guard's van can be seen at the end of the cutting in the picture on the right as No. 6001 **King Edward VII** comes out of Leamington with the 15.00 Birmingham-Paddington express. Half an hour later No. 2851 takes the West loop for Stratford-upon-Avon at Hatton Station and passes 'Austerity' 2-8-0 No. 90238 held at the signals before joining the main line with an up freight.

6 April 1957

Built in 1950 well after nationalisation, No. 7919 **Runter Hall** is working very hard as it approaches Twyford with a down Worcester express. The modified 'Halls' were fitted with plate frames and these extend above the running plate.

13 April 1957

Firemen at work!

No. 6004 **King George III** nears the end of its journey with the 07.00 Plymouth-Paddington express. A smoke effect of this sort was unusual coming out of Sonning Cutting as by this time the fireman would be taking things easy.

13 April 1957

18 At the west end of Sonning Cutting the sun has finally come through to light the spring foliage on the trees at the top of the bank. After the winter a day like this is a real tonic, although the crew on 2-6-2T No. 6113 (with a suburban train from Reading to London) do not appear to be taking advantage of the fresh air.

13 April 1957

19 Beyond Reading West Station the up 'Cornish Riviera Limited' approaches slowly as the signals are against it for the road through Reading General Station. No. 6025 **King Henry III** has come up from Plymouth, and the other two photographers are furiously winding on the film to take photographs as the train goes away.

13 April 1957

One never obtains perfection in railway photography and this picture could well do without the telegraph pole emerging from the top feed casing on the boiler of No. 6010 **King Charles I**. However the majesty and power is well portrayed, as the driver snaps open the regulator just after passing Reading West Station with the 15.30 Paddington-Penzance and starts the climb up to Savernake. The kitchen car leading the train would come off at Newton Abbot.

13 April 1957

21

One of the most interesting excursions undertaken by No. 3440 **City of Truro** was the 'Daffodil Express' organised by Ian Allan. 'Castle'-hauled from Paddington to Gloucester, 2-6-0 No. 4358 and **City of Truro** took the train on through the Welsh Valleys to Newport. Both engines are shown being prepared at Gloucester shed with the shed staff wearing the usual cycle clips to stop dust and dirt from getting up their trouser legs!

18 May 1957

22 The 'Daffodil Express' leaves Gloucester for Hereford in brilliant sunshine and complete with the ex-Devon Belle Observation Car. The 'Mogul' is painted and lined out in green livery.

18 May 1957

23 The train emerges from a tunnel near Mitcheldean Road Station on the single line some 5 miles from Ross-on-Wye. If only these pictures could be in colour you would see clearly the magnificent paintwork and lining on **City of Truro** together with the intricate G.W.R. scroll on the tender.

18 May 1957

24 A view looking West on the side of the valley near Pontypool showing a motley collection of goods wagons with wooden sides. An Auto-train is on its way down to Newport and a 66XX class 0-6-2T shunts in the yard.

18 May 1957

25 0-4-2T No. 1455 stands at Monmouth (Troy) waiting to leave with an Auto-train for Ross-on-Wye. Note the stone station building and the primitive water column. Beyond the short tunnel, the line used to go to Raglan and Usk to join the main Hereford-Newport line at Little Mill Junction.

18 May 1957

26   When the 'Daffodil Express' arrived at Crumlin Viaduct, due to weight restrictions **City of Truro** ran forward light (see left) and No. 4358 (above) comes into Crumlin Station with the train. After joining together again the train leaves for Neath (below). Crumlin Viaduct (now demolished) was built to carry double track at a height of 200 ft. across the valley and at a cost of £62,000. It was opened on 1 June 1857.

18 May 1957

27 Two miles south of Newport 2-8-0T No. 5215 has a mixed freight of scrap metal and oil wagons. In the distance can be seen the Newport Transporter Bridge across the River Usk and a ship in the docks.
18 May 1957

28 An up freight train behind 2-8-0T No. 4203 at the same location is seen on the relief line, with a train of oil wagons. This engine was built in 1912 and withdrawn in 1961. Note this early engine in the 42XX class had inside steam pipes. The 'barrier wagons' separating the engine and guards van from the train were to avoid fire risk when petrol was being carried.
18 May 1957

29 On the skyline can be seen the hills beyond the south coast of the Bristol Channel, as the 'Daffodil Express' gleaming in the low evening sunshine, approaches Newport for a further engine change. No. 4090 **Dorchester Castle**, (the second 'Castle' to receive a double chimney) took the train on to Paddington, during which a speed of 94 m.p.h. was achieved.
18 May 1957

30 No. 6014 **King Henry VII** rounds the curve just to the south of Tyseley Station with the 09.00 Birmingham-Paddington express. The North Warwick line from Stratford-upon-Avon to Birmingham can be seen coming in from the left of the picture and the two relief lines have now been removed.

22 May 1957

31 The standard heavy goods engines of the G.W.R. and L.N.W.R. are shown here with 2-8-0 No. 3811 on the left. An 0-8-0 No. 49417 comes through Leamington with a brick train from Whittlesey to Worcester having just used the connecting line at Leamington Spa South Junction signal box. In my boyhood days the sound of these engines with their Joy's valve gear ascending the bank at night betwen Leamington and Kenilworth, was music to the ears. No. 49417 was built at Crewe in 1921 as a member of the L.N.W.R. 'G.2' class, the last development of the 0-8-0 goods engine first built by Webb in 1892.

1 June 1957

32 This picture emphasises the 30 inch stroke of the 'Hall' class with the crosshead just starting its forward travel down the long crosshead guides. No. 4954 **Plaish Hall** is half way up Hatton Bank and the fireman's shovel is loaded, although it looks as if he may be at work with the pricker as this fire iron is leaning on one of the tool boxes.

25 May 1957

Two of a kind !

33 It is quite a coincidence that two trains with the same class of engine should pass each other within ten minutes of the same place in Sonning Cutting (Above) 2-6-2T No. 6129 is on its way to London while No. 6115 will shortly shut off steam for the Reading stop.
(Below) The driver of No. 4935 **Ketley Hall** screams a yell of delight as he heads for Paddington to pass No. 5932 **Haydon Hall** with a westbound semi-fast.

11 June 1957

34   2-8-0 No. 2801 stands outside Swindon Works with part of the foundry in the background. It was probably its last overhaul, as it was withdrawn at the end of the following year. Note the 'Shunters' gig' coupled to an ex-Taff Vale Railway 0-6-2T. The box on top of the 'Gig' contained a selection of ropes, sprags and re-railing ramps often required during shunting operations.

16 June 1957

35   In the present state of the railway relic market these chimneys are worth a fortune. An interesting exercise is guessing to which class of engine they belong. I think the chimney on the left is from a 'King' class.

16 June 1957

36   Outshopped with the final form of double chimney, No. 6017 **King Edward IV** awaits its first steaming the following day.

16 June 1957

37 There is quite a collection of bits and pieces here, from the fire irons to the railcar in the background. Perhaps the 4-wheel Dean brake 3rd and 40′ passenger brake van should catch your eye instead of the engines. However 0-6-0PT No. 2134 is of interest, as under B.R. it was transferred to the Midland Region for work in Birkenhead Docks and was probably fitted with a bell. It was also the last of the '2021' class to be withdrawn a month before this photograph was taken.

16 June 1957

11 June 1957

38 A special train returning from Swindon to Birmingham climbs Hatton Bank in the evening light. Unfortunately my camera was misbehaving and did not record correctly the magnificent smoke effect promised by the fireman during our conversation at Swindon.

16 June 1957

39 Passing the L.N.W.R. signal box at Saltney Junction, No. 1008 **County of Cardigan** joins the North Wales main line for the run into Chester General Station with the Margate to Birkenhead train. The hills of Wales can be seen in the background and are in fact the Ruabon Mountains.
27 June 1957

40 At Brombourgh between Chester and Birkenhead, the lorries of D & H Williams Coal and Coke Merchants are loading up from wagons parked in the siding. A permanent way gang are at work on the track with a ballast train hauled by 2-6-0 No. 78057, standing beyond the signal box. On the down main No. 6841 **Marlas Grange** (running tender first) has a mixed freight for Birkenhead. Note the observation blisters on each side of the signal box.
24 June 1957

41 No. 7827 **Lydham Manor** (now being restored to former glory on the Dart Valley Railway), approaches Chester with the 12.45 Pwllheli to Chester express. A Southern Region luggage van leads the train. I wonder how many model railways portray the supporting wires for their tall signals as shown in this picture.
27 June 1957

42 Another picture taken in the cutting south of Chester beyond the river Dee. A train for Manchester, on the North Wales main line, leaves the picture on the left as 2-6-0 No. 6339 approaches Saltney Junction with a train for Shrewsbury. The engine is shedded at Croes Newydd and the clean appearance should be noted. Full lining out was introduced as late as February 1957 for this class of engine.

27 June 1957

43 Approaching the City walls of Chester, No. 4092 **Dunraven Castle** nears the end of its journey from Wolverhampton with the 14.10 Paddington-Birkenhead express. The fireman is washing down the coal in the tender and getting the footplate clean and tidy before the next call of duty.

27 June 1957

44 Modified 'Hall' No. 6961 **Stedham Hall** passes Fosse Box at speed with a Boy Scouts special from London to Sutton Coldfield. This was on the occasion of the Jubilee celebrations, attended by scouts from all over the world.

11 August 1957

45 Even the cat looks at the trains and, being a black one, it certainly brought me luck for the next few days in clean engines and sunshine. Passing the Promenade at Dawlish with the 13.20 Penzance-Paddington express No. 5066 **Sir Felix Pole** looks as if it had recently been through Swindon Works. Notice in those days most of the cars were painted black; an unusual sight today!

24 August 1957

46 Southern engines were used between Exeter and Plymouth on the Great Western, to keep their drivers in training should their own route through Okehampton be closed for any reason. 'West Country Pacific No. 34001 **Exeter** leaves Dawlish with the 17.45 Exeter-Plymouth stopping train. A 'Siphon G' ventilated milk van is followed by a 'Siphon J' insulated milk van at the front of the train.
24 August 1957

47 It is interesting to see how few people are looking at No. 7000 **Viscount Portal** pulling out of the station heading towards Newton Abbot. I like the Box Brownie user in characteristic pose taking the annual holiday snaps!
24 August 1957

48 The following morning taken from the other side of the line as No. 5011 **Tintagel Castle** slows for the Dawlish stop, with a heavy load of 13 bogies.

25 August 1957

49 Kingswear Station can be picked out in the background as No. 6815 **Frilford Grange** passes Brittania Halt with a local train for Exeter. It is just starting the climb of 1 in 66 to Churston on the single line branch. The steam operated paddle car ferry was replaced by the present diesel model in 1960 and the two pieces of scrap metal in the water on the left are lying there today.

26 August 1957

50 Both these photographs are appropriate in view of the Torbay Steam Railway operation due to commence at the time of writing. 2-6-2T No. 5542 travels slowly down the branch with a British Rail built inspection saloon No. W 80976. The engine was one of a number fitted with automatic staff changing apparatus for working the Minehead and Barnstaple branches, but this was later removed.

26 August 1957

51 A general view of Laira shed (83D) taken from the road bridge carrying the A38 into Plymouth. The up train behind No. 5934 **Kneller Hall** comes down the 1 in 77 gradient with 8 coaches ready to tackle Hemerdon Bank unaided. On shed can be seen a variety of Great Western engines from 'Kings' down to '1361' class 0-6-0T.

28 August 1957

52 Dartmoor National Park begins beyond the main line, and this photograph taken from the A38 shows 'Battle of Britain' Pacific No. 34061 **73 Squadron** leaving Bittaford Halt on its way to Plymouth, with a train of very varied coaching stock.

28 August 1957

53

A magnificent sight with a set of chocolate and cream stock, the up 'Cornish Riviera Limited' crosses Blackford Viaduct behind No. 7813 **Freshford Manor** and No. 6021 **King Richard II**.

28 August 1957

54 The carriage boards read Plymouth, Bristol, Shrewsbury and Manchester (London Road)' and the time is around 14.00 so the time table fanatics can work out which train is being hauled by No. 5048 **Earl of Devon** as it approaches South Brent.
28 August 1957

55 No. 8451 was built by the Yorkshire Engine Company in 1949 and the sharper lip on the copper-capped chimney can be compared with those engines of the same class built at Swindon. Carying a Newton Abbot shed plate, it is in a remarkable state of cleanliness as it passes Wrangaton Station heading towards Plymouth with a brake van.
28 August 1957

56 No. 6017 **King Edward IV** slows to 5 m.p.h. between South Brent and Wrangaton for permanent way work being carried out on the down main line. The curved arch metal road bridge taking a country lane across the line should be of interest to modellers.
28 August 1957

57 For the Great Western enthusiast this picture has a wealth of detail from the buildings, signalling and station layout. The name board 'South Brent (change for the Kingsbridge Branch)' is seen on the left platform complete with palm trees, and 4077 **Chepstow Castle** is coming through with the up 'Royal Duchy'. As a child I often wondered why the passenger footbridge should be fitted with frosted glass!

28 August 1957

58

2-6-2T No. 5533 comes into Brent Station with the branch train from Kingsbridge. The main line to Totnes disappears round the corner hugging the south edge of Dartmoor.

28 August 1957

59 Climbing the 1 in 46 bank between Totnes and Tigley Box, an unidentified train from Paddington to Plymouth has two 'Castles' in charge, No. 5064 **Bishops Castle** and No. 7022 **Hereford Castle.** The 107 reporting number covered the 07.30 Paddington-Paignton express so probably **Bishops Castle** came on at Newton Abbot.

28 August 1957

60 No. 4978 **Westwood Hall** and No. 1000 **County of Middlesex** drop into Totnes with a Royal Mail Coach leading. The Post Office Mail pick-up apparatus can be seen beside the sixth coach. The 'County' still retains the original shape of double chimney with which it was built.

28 August 1957

61 These three photographs were taken at the top of Dainton Bank where the main line disappears into a short tunnel. 2-8-0 No. 2875 is working very hard with a down freight. Note the engine is blowing off and 2-6-2T No. 5196 acting as banker, has already shut off steam before the tunnel mouth is reached. The cheerful guard will shortly be jumping into action pinning down brakes before the descent to Totnes the other side of the tunnel.

28 August 1957

62 A general view of Newton Abbot Station in the evening, with 2-6-0 No. 6385 leaving for Torquay. This engine, together with No. 6372 (fully lined out in green and polished safety valve covers) was used for working the Royal Train on 8 May 1956 from Taunton to Barnstaple. Note the locomotive weather cock beyond the shed the water tank depicting a broad gauge engine.
28 August 1957

63 After working the down 'Torbay Express' from Paddington, No. 5008 **Raglan Castle** returns to Newton Abbot shed with a freight train from Kingswear.
28 August 1957

64 I have included this picture taken at the well known sea wall beyond Teignmouth Station as it portrays all the feelings of a hot summer day. No. 5028 **Llantilio Castle** is in charge of the 07.30 Penzance to Crewe express.
29 August 1957

65 It was unusual to find a single chimney 'King' in charge of the up 'Royal Duchy' at the end of the summer in 1957, as there were only 8 engines not rebuilt with double chimney. I like this picture as there is no headboard or reporting numbers and the level angle shows off the pleasing lines of No. 6029 **King Edward VIII** followed by an immaculate rake of chocolate and cream stock.

29 August 1957

66 2-8-0 No. 3853 shedded at Severn Tunnel Junction and sporting a clean black livery, joins the River Teign for its journey up to Newton Abbot with a short freight train. It is almost high tide and you can see the bridge carying the road from Teignmouth to Shaldon in the background with Teignmouth docks beyond.

29 August 1957

67 We now look upstream with 2-6-0 No. 6385 disappearing towards Newton Abbot and No. 6002 **King William IV** shutting off steam for the curves through Teignmouth with the 'Up Limited'. Note the milepost just about to disappear from view behind the engine.

29 August 1957

68 Perhaps a rather distracting background, but I liked the sweep of the stone embankment and the splendid old wooden barge which I believe was a primitive drilling rig for checking the river bed. The driver of No. 6008 **King James II** has just opened the regulator after passing through Teignmouth with the down 'Cornish Riviera Limited'.

29 August 1957

69 I covered 96,000 miles in the Morris Minor and sixteen years later it is still running around Coventry. Powderham Castle is across the fields to the left and the estuary of the River Exe behind the trees. No. 5054 **Earl of Ducie** comes round the curve with the down 'Royal Duchy'.
29 August 1957

70

Great Western glass lined milk tanks and gas cylinder wagons make up this lightweight train behind No. 7914 **Lleweni Hall** as it heads North near Starcross.
29 August 1957

71 No. 6017 **King Edward IV** approaches Parson's Tunnel signal box with the 07.30 Truro-Paddington express. I was to meet, at Shrewsbury later the following month, the enthusiast leaning out of the second carriage who evidently must have remembered my face or was it the large camera I carried?
30 August 1957

Turning round from the previous picture is a typical Great Western scene, it was taken on a brilliant sunny morning, with No. 4920 **Dumbleton Hall** (shedded at Taunton) making for the West past the signal box which is now sadly no longer with us. It must have been a pleasant occupation working that box in the summer or living in the house on the hill watching the trains go by.

30 August 1957

No. 5078 **Beaufort** has a modest load of 10 bogies on the up 'Torbay Express'. From the viewpoint near Dawlish the train can be seen further round the coast and by looking at the sky it is possible to calculate if a cloud will obscure the sun when the train arrives. A nasty black shadow creeps up the track and envelopes the rear coaches. Lucky on this occasion!!

30 August 1957

74 Down in the 'dip' between Leamington and Warwick, the Autumn excursion to Swindon Works and Sheds by the Midland Area of the Stephenson Locomotive Society returns to Birmingham Snow Hill behind No. 3440 **City of Truro**. Note the temporary shortened safety valve cover which was put on after an accident with the taller version.

1 September 1957

75 The signal at the east end of Twyford Station makes this picture, as No. 5095 **Barbury Castle** passes through with the 07.43 Cardiff to Paddington express. The main line snaking its way towards Sonning Cutting may be seen above the footbridge beyond which on the right side are visible the signals of the branch coming in from Henley-on-Thames.

7 September 1957

76 Twyford Station has a liberal collection of gas lamps and a strong west wind blows a mantle of steam forward from the safety valves of No. 4996 **Eden Hall** as it waits with a parcels train, on the up relief line. 'Brittania' Pacific No. 70022 **Tornado** is shedded at Cardiff Canton and left Newport at 08.20 arriving in Paddington at 10.50.

7 September 1957

77
Broadside view of No. 6003 **King George IV** speeding past Twyford signal box with the 09.30 Paddington-Plymouth express. The fireman is probably cleaning the footplate or adjusting the ashpan dampers.
7 September 1957

78
In the later years of steam the '4700' class were often pressed into service for the summer timetable. This picture shows No. 4700 with a West Country express bound for Paddington entering Sonning Cutting. This particular engine in fully lined out livery attended the Darlington Railway Centenary celebrations in 1925.
7 September 1957

79 No. 6000 **King George V** eases forward towards Reading West Station waiting for the signals to clear while working the 10.00 Newquay-Paddington express. The delay was caused by No. 30783 **Sir Gillemere** using the west triangle at Reading with a through train from the North to the South coast, changing engines at Oxford. It can be seen disappearing under the far roadbridge.

7 September 1957

80 After a turn round at Paddington of 55 minutes No. 70022 **Tornado** returns to South Wales with the 13.55 Paddington-Pembroke Dock seen here passing No. 5974 **Wallsworth Hall** in Sonning Cutting.

7 September 1957

81 Two electrically operated distant signals stand over Goring water troughs as No. 5027 **Farleigh Castle** sweeps by with the 17.05 Paddington-Weston-Super-Mare express. This was always a difficult and restricted place for picture taking, but this one has more than usual feeling of movement, emphasised by the low angle of the sun and a good smoke effect.

7 September 1957

82 Shedded at Cardiff Canton No. 6939 **Calveley Hall** leaves Leamington on the climb up to Harbury with the Sunday 'Cornishman'.

8 September 1957

83 Now with a tall safety valve cover reinstated, No. 3440 **City of Truro** approaches Shrewsbury with the Talyllyn Railway special train from Paddington to Towyn. The first coach is of interest being a 70 ft Tribog Compo with 1st, 2nd and 3rd class lavatories.

28 September 1957

84 Inspector Holland on the left with the Shedmaster at Shrewsbury stand in front of L & Y 2-4-2T No. 50781 which they prepared for the special. The engines are in the G.W.R. part of the shed complex, with an inspection pit in the foreground.

28 September 1957

85 The crews wave from the cabs as the train, now on its way from Shrewsbury to Towyn, has just passed the fixed distant signal guarding the approach to Abermule Station. The 'Dukedog' is No. 9021 somewhat obscured by the haze of smoke from the leading engine. What enormous springs the L & Y engine has compared with the Dukedog.

28 September 1957

86 Here is a level crossing gate guarding the Cambrian main line where it is crossed by the main road from Welshpool to Aberystwyth. Apart from the fixed distant signal that lovely cast right-angled supporting bracket above the hinges of the gate is worthy of study by modellers.

28 September 1957

87

No. 7828 **Odney Manor** takes the up 'Cambrian Coast Express' out of Caers Station on its way to London with an engine change at Shrewsbury. Note the Cambrian Railway signal with wooden arm.
28 September 1957

88

After leaving Moat Lane Junction both engines are working very hard on the climb to Talerddig summit, and in this picture are seen passing Pontdolgoch Station with the weather clouding over as the Welsh Hills are approached.

28 September 1957

89

On arriving at Towyn with rain in the hills, 0-6-0 No. 2239 shuts off steam for the station and is shown passing the wharf of the Talyllyn railway.

28 September 1957

90

No. 7000 **Viscount Portal** heads the down Torbay Express between Slough and Taplow, and obscures a London bound coal train from South Wales.

5 October 1957

91

No. 6005 **King George II** has just passed Seer Green Station and is on the falling gradient to Gerrards Cross. Probably travelling over 80 m.p.h., the train is the 10.00 Birmingham Snow Hill-Paddington express with a solitary Great Western coach travelling in style next to the tender. Note all the flies and dirt stuck on the front of the outside cylinder covers.

5 October 1957

All these three pictures were taken between Slough and Taplow. No. 4995 **Easton Hall** is on the down main line with a semi-fast for Reading.

5 October 1957

93

'The Red Dragon' hauled by 'Brittania' Pacific No. 70023 **Venus** makes for London. Perhaps the purist would disapprove of these engines being included but they were part of the scene and a very good one at that—handsome looking machines.

5 October 1957

94

There appears to be some trouble with the 'Hall' class engine as both the crew are looking over the side. A returning empty milk train headed by 2-6-0 No. 5398 is on the down relief line. Note the G.W. on the tender of the 'Hall'.

5 October 1957

95 This station no longer exists today like so many others, but the layout is typical with concrete lamp posts and a winding mechanism for hauling up the Tilley lamps in the evening. No. 6020 **King Henry IV** climbs the 1 in 779 through Southam Road and Harbury Station with the 11.35 Wolverhampton-Paddington express.
14 October 1957

96 This appears to be an unusual situation as 'Stanier' 2-8-0 No. 48686 comes out of the sidings betwen the two stations at Leamington and heads a Nuneaton coal train for the South. No. 5070 **Sir Daniel Gooch** will have to wait at least ten minutes before the freight reaches Fosse Box Siding. Known as 'the Up Cheap' Wolverhampton-Paddington (via Oxford) it stopped in Leamington from 14.16 to 14.38, and originated from early days when few trains ran carrying 3rd class passengers and stopped at every station.
21 December 1957

97 This picture is full of material for the modeller and is a view taken from the cattle pens beside the down goods sidings at Leamington Spa. No. 6959 **Peatling Hall** heads towards Birmingham with an early morning train, as the 0-6-0PT shunting in the exchange sidings takes on water. The Avenue Station signal box is visible behind the water column.
2 November 1957

98 The 09.10 Paddington-Birkenhead express nears the top of Hatton Bank behind No. 6009 **King Charles II**. The coaches include the standard cream and red livery, Great Western chocolate and cream, and the standard maroon shown on the seventh vehicle.

2 November 1957

99 Further down the bank No. 7030 **Cranbrook Castle** heads the 'Cambrian Coast Express' on its way to Aberystwyth and Pwllheli. The down goods line and all signalling have now been removed.

2 November 1957

the run leaves Warwick goods yard and is shown passing the Cape ground frame on the right of the picture. The individual 'puffs' can clearly be seen as the driver gets away slowly to avoid snatching the couplings. Cleaning marks show up clearly on the tender.

2 November 1957

101 The low sun on a December morning reflects from the tender of No. 6001 **King Edward VII** as it passes Warwick Gas Works with the 11.10 Paddington-Birkenhead express. This photograph shows the bogie design with its inside and outside bearings for the wheels and the dished main frames.

21 December 1957

'Neck and neck' but not for long as No. 70019 **Lightning** sweeps by 2-6-0 No. 5381 on a freight for London. The location is between Maidenhead and Twyford.
1 March 1958

Later in the afternoon No. 7010 **Avondale Castle** passes Ruscombe Box and into the only ray of sunshine on that particular day as it heads for Paddington.
There always seems to be a bicycle beside the steps leading up to signal boxes where the signalman can be seen at work.
1 March 1958

Slowed down by a permanent way slack in Southam Road and Harbury Station, No. 5032 **Usk Castle** accelerates the 11.10 Paddington-Birkenhead express through Harbury Cutting and underneath a farmers road bridge which needs some drastic repairs carried out to the brickwork.
8 March 1958

105

Hatton Junction is just round the corner and, with a strong southerly gale blowing, 0-6-0PT No. 9429 is working a local train from Leamington to Stratford-upon-Avon and Worcester.

22 March 1958

106

The only days I could see the 'Bristolian' was during annual holidays or the Tuesday of the Easter and Whitsun holiday. This is the up train on the Easter Tuesday and is taken from the North end at Cholsey and Moulsford Station. Signal wires and point rodding abound in the late dusk with a colour light showing below the arm of the signal beyond the train. The exposure was 1/250 at f4 on HP3 film and the engine is No. 7015 **Carn Brea Castle**.

8 April 1958

107 A late afternoon picture at the entrance to Old Oak Common and looking towards Paddington. A 2-6-2T has a stopping train to Reading while a '9400' class 0-6-0PT approaches for the carriage sidings. A 'King' disappears up the flyover and a class 5 No. 45135 works tender first with a freight on the line from Willesden - Kensington Olympia and the Southern Region. Note the trolley bus above the first coach of the local train.

12 April 1958

108 2-6-2T No. 6103 makes for Reading with an evening commuter train as a set of empty stock are hauled up the flyover to reach the down side of the main line. A peculiar mixture of Gas Works, tombstones and car tyres dominate the background to the east of Old Oak Common.

12 April 1958

109

After a day's work coming up from Kingswear with the 'Torbay Express', No. 7004 **Eastnor Castle** has backed down from Paddington and awaits the signals for moving into Old Oak Common Shed. The Grand Union Canal runs along behind the brick wall and well above track level.

12 April 1958

110 The 'Cathedrals Express' headed by No. 7007 **Great Western** passes by and, with the sun head on in the West, the spit and polish on the smoke-box glistens on this immaculate Worcester engine a few minutes after leaving Paddington.

12 April 1958

111 Nearing the top of Gresford Bank, (a climb of 1 in 82½) No. 7800 **Torquay Manor** will soon be stopping at Wrexham General Station with a local train from Chester.

26 April 1958

112

0-6-0PT No. 5416 has shut off steam for the Ruabon stop with an Auto-train most likely stopping at all stations between Wrexham and Oswestry. The engine is painted green and fully lined out together with polished safety valve bonnet, and the signals are worthy of note.

26 April 1958

113

This magnificent viaduct spans the Vale of Llangollen and the River Dee flows beneath. No. 5957 **Hutton Hall** with Southern stock is hauling the 09.20 Birkenhead to Bournemouth West express via Oxford and Reading West.

26 April 1958

114

Originally built in 1932 as No. 9308, the 'Mogul' was renumbered as late as June the year before this picture was taken. These were the last of the G.W.R. 'Moguls' and were fitted with side window cabs, screw reverse and outside steam pipes. Note the tall safety valve bonnet.

At the junction with the Llangollen line south of Ruabon, No. 7330 has a steam breakdown crane in tow.

26 April 1958

115

Slowing down for the end of its journey from Paddington to Ruabon, No. 3440 **City of Truro** hauls an eight coach load of members of the Festiniog Railway Society. The sun shone and the 'City' positively glistens in the spring light, but alas the driver shut off steam just before the bridge. The first coach is a clean example of G.W. toplight brake 1st. The two coaches following are Craven built prototype first and second class open coaches and two prototype second class open vehicles built at Doncaster.

26 April 1958

116   After an engine change at Ruabon the F.R.S. special travels on to Minff-
ordd via Corwen and Dolgellau. Both photographs were taken from the
roadside of the A5 and show No. 9017 (now on the Bluebell line) and
No. 9021 working on the single line. In the bottom picture the Llantysilio
Mountains dominate the scene and the sun miraculously comes through
to sparkle on the clear water of the River Dee. Inspector Holland con-
tinues to wave.

26 April 1958

117 This could be classed as an interloper, but after all the 'Duke' did undergo test on the Western Region and this is the only time I saw it in clean condition. It is seen leaving Crewe with a 'Trains Illustrated' special. The dark sky is a torrential storm sweeping over Crewe and, as luck would have it, the sun was shining as the train came past Basford Hall Junction signal box on its way to Euston with the ex-'Devon Belle' observation car at the rear.

118 This is the first picture taken on my final visit to the West Country by car on a very dull day. An early start from home was necessary, to meet up with the down 'Bristolian' betwen Didcot and Steventon. No. 6015 **King Richard III** was travelling very fast on a rising gradient and for a moment the sun came through the clouds as the train swept by.

19 May 1958

119 Driving on further south, I came to Newbury to see the down 'Cornish Riviera Express' come through the station behind No. 6004 **King George III**. 2-6-0 No. 7317 waits with a freight in the platform. Note the water tank set up on the bank away from the track.

19 May 1958